THE EMPOWERING PARENT

A Practical Guide to Unlocking the Potential in Your Child

David C Hall

RETHINK PRESS

First published in Great Britain in 2019 by Rethink Press
(www.rethinkpress.com)

Cover image © Jesse Gerald Photography

Contents

Introduction

At the tender age of three, I was diagnosed with dyslexia. During the 1980s most children with dyslexia were statemented. Compared to my peers I made slow progress, which significantly impacted my confidence. My class consisted of eight children, one lead teacher and a teaching assistant but I struggled with my schoolwork and would regularly become frustrated. Little did I know this would forge in me a resilience that would become a foundation for success.

In Year 6, I achieved level 2b on my SATs. This meant I was underachieving by four school years in relation to my peers. With supportive parents and the motivation to succeed, I developed a routine, a strong work ethic and the confidence needed to set and achieve goals. This paved the way for my academic success, and I left secondary school with ten GCSE passes at A* to C.

I am now a qualified science teacher with over eleven years of teaching experience. My philosophy is that your child can succeed, no matter what their story. Whether they're dealing with behaviour challenges at school, lack of concentration or underachievement, I can work with them to unlock their potential: to help them become a happy and confident learner, meet and exceed school targets and pursue a career aligned with their gifts and talents. I've distilled my personal challenges and the information I've learned over the years into principles and strategies that will unlock the potential in your child. I can help them improve by a whole grade in a school year.

The Empowering Parent is divided into three sections.

Section One

This section deals with the importance of creating an empowering environment for your child. There are two ingredients in an empowering environment: connection and cultivation. These ingredients underpin the three parenting models: the Free-for-all Parenting Model, the Disempowering Parenting Model and the Empowering Parenting Model.

Section one offers practical strategies for creating an empowering environment for children through the Empowering Parenting Model. An empowering environment is key to raising children who have high emotional intelligence, which in turn will raise their intelligence quotient (IQ).

Section Two

This section deals with how a tutor can unlock potential in your child. It explores effective learning strategies, tips for finding the tutor of your dreams and the best ways to navigate the education system.

Section Three

This section focuses on the Purpose Model, which will enable your child to have a gift- and talent-orientated career.

To effectively unlock potential in your child, it's important to have a support system and to use education as a tool for empowerment.

This section also addresses how lasting success isn't solely based on gifts or talents, but on work ethic. A strong work ethic allows children to make a lasting impact with their gifts and talents. And a strong work ethic is underpinned by strategic planning.

THE EMPOWERING ENVIRONMENT

Throughout history, humans have understood that environment is paramount to not only surviving, but also flourishing.

A child's environment is key to their development. Children are a reflection of their household environments. Are you creating an environment in which your child can flourish? If you aren't, don't lose hope. This race is not for the swift. What's most important in this race is finishing. We all make mistakes. Mistakes are an opportunity to review what we've been doing and figure out how we can improve.

An empowering environment is one that fosters transformation through connection and cultivation. It is the basis for raising happy and confident children, and the foundation of accelerated academic progress.

So how do you create an empowering environment in which your child can thrive? Let's explore this.

ONE

Connection

We all have an innate need to be loved and to love others. And all parents are responsible for ensuring the environment in their household allows for this kind of connection.

It's well known that for every effect there is a cause. The right kind of household environment (the cause) will impact your child's behaviour (effect). A child's behaviour is always an insight into their psychology. To connect with your child on an emotional level, it's important to understand their psychology.

Unlocking Potential framework

This framework to unlock potential is made up of six principles. If executed properly, these principles will unlock your child's potential.

1. **Patience.** Patience is the ability to proactively wait for your child to come around. It involves communicating to your child what you expect from them without becoming irritated. Patience is the ability to speak the truth to your child in a way that is empowering.

   Words are containers of the expression of your thoughts. These containers are either dis-empowering thoughts (limiting thoughts) or empowering thoughts. What are you speaking to your children? Do the words you speak to your children build emotional resilience, confidence, healthy self-esteem and an 'I can do' attitude? Or do they leave your child emotionally depleted, and lower their confidence or self-esteem?

In the heat of the moment, the quality of patience will enable you to speak empowering words to your child, giving them a sense of emotional security, belonging and hope.

How can you demonstrate patience to your child?

2. **Kindness.** Kindness means serving your children by sincerely volunteering your gifts, your talents, your time and your resources. Kindness is a state of being, one which always asks the questions: How can I serve my children to unlock their potential? How can my gifts, my talents, my time and my resources be used to unlock my children's potential?

3. **Humility.** Humility is being able to recognise your own values, and others', while acknowledging the need for guidance in your developmental areas.

   Humility is the quality in which you are able to demonstrate correction. In other words, if your child corrected you, how would you feel? Would you feel a sense of embarrassment? Or would you receive the correction with appreciation?

   Our age does not necessarily mean we know it all, rather the quality of humility understands interdependence. Together we can achieve more.

   How have you demonstrated humility when interacting with your child?

4. **Forgiveness.** Forgiveness is an intentional decision to release anger and resentment towards someone who has hurt you. Someone once said: 'it takes a village to raise a child'. If your relationships with

people in your support network are strained because forgiveness is needed and hasn't been given, the well-being of your child will be negatively affected, directly or indirectly.

Forgiveness is a great strategy of guarding your mind. Your mind is the seat in which either positive or negative emotions will find expression in your life.

In fact, science has demonstrated lack of forgiveness as a potential cause of becoming sick, ie phychosomatic disorder.

Since children are sponges of their environment, the very emotions we can carry will be picked up by our children. We have a duty of care to ensure we provide an empowering environment for our children. In other words, our emotional well-being as parents will either dis-empower our children or empower them.

I encourage you today, if there is someone you have not forgiven, please seek out the necessary support to begin the process of forgiveness. You will feel better for it, and so will your children.

Who can you forgive today?

5. **Courtesy.** Put simply, courtesy is politeness. Parents' behaviour behind closed doors is what truly influences a child's behaviour in public. It's vital to model courteous behaviour at home.

When last have you demonstrated courteous behaviour in front of your child?

Do you demand your child obey your requests? Or do you ask your children politely? Would you go to an apple tree bearing oranges? Or would you go to an orange tree bearing apples? The answer is no!

What am I saying is that you cannot expect your children to show courtesy to you as parents and others, if you have not first modelled courteous behaviour to your children and to others.

6. **Parenting psychology.** Your parenting psychology shapes your behaviour as a parent. If you don't like your child's behaviour, you need to look at the behaviour you're modelling. Children mirror their household environment.

The Unlocking Potential framework will help you learn your child's communication preference. Each child perceives love in a unique way, and each child prefers to receive it in a unique way – either through praise, a prize or participation. This is their Unlocking Potential Communication Preference.

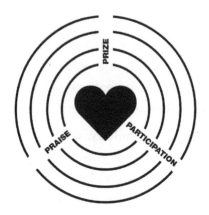

1. Praise: affirming your child's good qualities, gifts and talents

2. Prize: (a) buying your child presents aligned with their gifts, talents and interests; and (b) looking for opportunities to serve your child

3. Participation: (a) giving your child your undivided attention through conversation or activities; and (b) giving your child physical contact (eg hugs)

TWO

Cultivation

Unlocking potential involves not just connection but also cultivation. Cultivation is the outcome of discipline. Parents must cultivate positive character traits in their children.

I define cultivation as developing character excellence using a moral compass to ensure a code of behaviour is adhered to.

Cultivation is key when it comes to unlocking your child's potential. Whether your child is at the top of their class or displaying behaviour challenges or has excellent character but hasn't fully tapped into their potential, this can be changed.

Benefits of cultivating your child

1. Empowers children to use their moral compass: effective cultivation over time will empower your children to make ethical decisions.

2. Fosters emotional intelligence: effective cultivation helps children to not only become aware of their emotions but also to connect with these emotions and channel them in the right way.

3. Promotes self-discipline: one of the key ingredients of academic success is self-discipline. Research has demonstrated countless times that children who are

disciplined are more likely to develop intrinsic motivation.[1]

Three cornerstones of empowering cultivation

For cultivation to be empowering and trans-formational, three things must be considered:

1 Xiao, S X. 2016. Inductive Discipline and Children's Prosocial Behavior: the role of parental emotion regulation strategies. *Dissertations ALL.* Paper 507. https://surface.syr.edu/etd /507

1. **Parent-child relationship.** The parent-child relationship is the bedrock of cultivation. For cultivation to be effective, the parent-child bond must be strong. There needs to be a good balance of connection and cultivation. Research has demonstrated that when the parent-child relationship is vibrant, the child responds positively to cultivation.

2. **Positive behaviour strategies.** Remember, a child's behaviour is always a mirror reflection of their psychology. Positive reinforcement is a great tool to encourage the behaviour you want to cultivate. Through positive reinforcement, you can cultivate a desirable character, gifts and talents in your child and communicate your expectations to them.

3. **Strategies for discouraging unwanted behaviours.** Consequences are great tools to help your children learn from their

mistakes, so they're empowered to make better choices in the future.

When giving your child consequences, you should:

- Make sure it's appropriate for their age, temperament and misbehaviour

- Communicate your expectations in advance, so your child is clear about why they are receiving a consequence

- Always treat your child with dignity and respect

THREE

The Purpose Of Parenting

Parents have a responsibility to do their best to raise children who become adults who are effectual – adults who display moral excellence and who positively contribute to society. As parents, we are impacting the next generation. If we don't like what we see in our world, we must inspire the change. And we can do so by focusing on the things in our sphere of influence.

Children are a gift, and they are within our sphere of influence. When children are born, they have a blank slate. What's written on their slate as they grow up is largely dependent on their immediate environment (ie the place in which they spend most of their time).

What are you writing on your child's slate? Is it transformational – unlocking their potential? Is it empowering? Does it communicate unconditional love? Does it convey that all things are possible with the right support?

Parents also have a responsibility to ensure that the writing on their child's slate not only empowers their child, but also transcends generations.

We must empower our children to attain excellence holistically – to be grounded in themselves but also relevant to their peers so they can one day be a positive contributor to society. We must educate them to be vibrant physically, socially, intellectually and morally.

Since children are sponges that soak up their environments, it's imperative to create and sustain a stimulating, nurturing, supportive and loving environment in the home.

Research has demonstrated time and again that the manner in which children are parented are indicators of the kind of children adults become. It's therefore important to use a parenting model that empowers your child. The right parenting model will unlock holistic potential and allow your child to discover their calling, gifts and talents, so they can live a fulfilled life.

PARENTING MODEL OVERVIEW

	FREE-FOR-ALL PARENTING MODEL	DISEMPOWERING PARENTING MODEL	EMPOWERING PARENTING MODEL
CULTIVATION	↓	↑	↑
CONNECTION	↑	↓	↑

Parenting Model Overview

23

FOUR

Free-For-All Parenting Model

How effectively we unlock potential in our children depends on the model we use to parent them.

The first one we'll look at is the Free-for-all Parenting Model. As shown in the diagram below, the free-for-all parent heavily relies on connection and limits cultivation.

Free-for-all Parenting Model

Indicators of free-for-all parenting

1. There will be no or limited rules for the child – the parent will frequently use bribery (eg food, toys or gifts) to encourage the behaviour they're seeking in their child.

2. The child will lack self-discipline due to a lack of routine.

3. The parent will see themselves as a friend to their child rather than a parent (eg they'll ask their child to make a decision that isn't age-appropriate).

Consequences of free-for-all parenting

1. **Underachievement.** Children who are parented by free-for-all parents tend to underachieve compared to their peers. This is largely due to their parents' lack of expectations for them.

2. **Poor time-management skills.** Free-for-all parents seldom embed family routines. Without routines, children don't learn the discipline to regulate themselves. This results in poor time-management skills.

3. **Poor decisions.** Free-for-all parents tend not to impart a moral compass in their children by way of cultivation, so the children may struggle to make the right decision (or it may take them a while to make the correct one).

4. **Delinquency.** Children raised by free-for-all parents have a higher risk of being delinquent due to lack of cultivation.

5. **Low emotional intelligence.** In the Free-for-all Parenting Model, children aren't encouraged to develop the capacity to manage their emotions. This means that in their adulthood, they're likely to struggle when faced with stressful situations.

FIVE

Disempowering Parenting Model

Using the Disempowering Parenting Model, parents focus on cultivation with little regard for connection. This creates an imbalance, as shown in the diagram below.

Disempowering Parenting Model

Indicators of disempowering parenting

1. Punishment is used as a form of cultivation. Punishment dives into the realm of 'what' but never explores the realm of 'why'. Parents who use this model tend to tell their children what they've done wrong but never discuss why the behaviour is wrong. The results of the punishment are largely rooted in fear and are short-lived.

2. Parents who use the Disempowering Parenting Model often encourage their children to pursue careers that will give them social and economic status ('keeping up with the Joneses'), rather than to pursue and unlock their natural talents and gifts.

3. Parents who adopt this model tend to believe that children should be seen and not heard. They seldom give their

children the opportunity to develop their independence by empowering them to make age-appropriate decisions.

4. These parents don't prioritise connection with their children on an emotional level. They rarely communicate their love for their child through the child's Unlocking Potential Communication Preference; rather, they focus on communicating their expectations, boundaries and rules.

Consequences of disempowering parenting

1. **Low self-esteem.** Parents who use the Disempowering Parenting Model are likely to raise children with low self-esteem. A child's self-esteem is created over time as a result of their interactions with their parents as well as life situations.

2. Children raised by disempowering parents tend to:

   – Have a negative outlook on life

   – Lack confidence

   – Focus on their weaknesses rather than their strengths

   – Find it difficult to accept recognition from others

   – Focus on what could go wrong in a situation

3. **Approval-seeking.** Children who are raised according to the Disempowering Parenting Model seek to earn their parents' approval through their obedience and their successes. They don't feel that their parents' love is unconditional.

4. **Anger.** Children with disempowering parents are likely to be more aggressive as a result of frustration. This frustration results from their feeling a lack of connection.

SIX

Empowering Parenting Model

Empowering parents enable their children to flourish in their transition into adulthood. This is because those who parent using the Empowering Parenting Model have a balanced view of connection and cultivation. They understand that to effectively cultivate their children, it's necessary to connect with them. They understand that with the right balance, they will build a strong, healthy and tenacious relationship with their children.

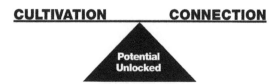

Empowering Parenting Model

Indicators of empowering parenting

1. A child parented by empowering parents will be encouraged to discover for themselves their unique blend of gifts and talents, and to use these to create a career that will enable them to serve the world.

2. They are also likely to have good self-esteem – their voice is heard, even if their parents don't agree with what they're saying.

3. Consequences are favoured over punishment. Again, punishment is a short-term measure, while consequences

are a long-term strategy. Empowering parents seek to understand the root cause of the child's misbehaviour, and they'll use consequences to bridge the gap between the misbehaviour and the desired behaviour.

4. A child raised by empowering parents will tend to be open to receiving consequences. They are clear about what their parents expect from them.

Benefits of empowering parenting

Children raised according to the Empowering Parenting Model are likely to:

1. Have high emotional intelligence, resulting in a higher IQ

2. Be good role models for others

3. Have good self-esteem

4. Be confident

5. Have good social skills

6. Be happier

Strategies to become an empowering parent

1. **Share your expectations.** Consult with your children and devise seven Unlocking Potential Rules. The purpose of these rules is to communicate to your children the expectations you have for your household. Including your children in the process will teach them about personal responsibility and accountability.

2. **Pre-determine consequences.** The basis of effective cultivation is consequences, not punishment. Punishment has a short-term benefit (rooted in fear) while consequences, when applied correctly,

will teach them valuable lessons in a supportive, nurturing and respectful way.

3. **Be consistent.** The purpose of cultivation is to empower your children to develop the quality that is lacking. This lack will always manifest itself behaviourally. Our role as parents is to cultivate our children through connection – you must find the balance between the two.

4. **Cultivate proactively.** Model the behaviour you wish to see in your child and always reinforce positive behaviour.

THE EMPOWERING STUDYING ENVIRONMENT

Seated at the Olympics games, the atmosphere is charged with anticipation of who will win! Countdown: 3, 2, 1, go! The audience is now concentrating on watching the athletes as they sprint around the stadium. The finish line is in sight, the atmosphere is now filled with greater excitement.

The athlete didn't just win the race. Authentic overnight success is the resulting compound effect of discipline, sacrifices, practice and a growth mindset. Every successful athlete understands the importance of hiring their own sports coach. Why you may ask? An athlete understands that a sport coach is needed to optimise their sport performance, necessary to win the race.

The purpose of a sports coach is to improve the performance of the athlete. A good coach always begins with the end in mind (the desired performance), reviews the athlete's current performance, ascertains the gap between the two and identifies a strategic plan to attain the desired performance.

Just like an athlete need a sports coach to optimise their performance, every child needs an empowering studying environment to optimise their academic performance. A good tutor assumes the role of a sports coach. They can provide advice on the strategies needed to maximise your child's learning potential and empower your child with a repertoire of resources that will not only improve their confidence but, over time, raise the grades.

SEVEN

Learning Success Is Predictable

Each year, the third Thursday of August is an unforgettable day for year elevens. This is the day they collect their General Certificate of Secondary Education (GCSE) – the *outcome* of a two-year course.

For some, the day is memorable for all the right reasons: they see their hard work clearly reflected in the grades they've attained. But others may feel their grades aren't representative of their full potential.

The outcome is a result of sequential compounding. In other words, the grade achieved is a result of competence, habits, practice and mindset. Every outcome can be traced back to mindset.

As shown in the diagram, our mindset is the collection of thoughts and beliefs we hold about ourselves. What we think, we become! It's important to understand that our mindset always influences our outcome.

When the correct mindset is executed with a harmonious corresponding method, you will see the formation of practice.

When you practice something repeatedly for at least twenty-one days, a habit is formed. And once a habit has been formed, you no longer need to consciously think about practising something. You just do it. Learning to drive a car is a good example. At first, driving requires serious thought (practice), but with regular practice, it becomes second nature.

Your new habit determines your level of competence, your ability to complete a task at a high level.

The outcome you see is the direct result of competence. The more competent we become at something, the more favourable our outcome, the result, will be. The result is largely impacted by our mindset.

It's important to acknowledge that your child's mindset will always mirror the environment you create for them.

Learning

I define learning as the acquisition of new knowledge or skills. There are three pillars of effective learning, shown in the diagram below: strategy, sessions and study.

For learning to be effective, there must be a learning strategy. The learning strategy sets out a goal and a plan of action for achieving the goal. This strategy underpins the learning session, where knowledge or skills are imparted. A study session is time allotted to reduce impact of the forgetting curve and simultaneously increase the learning curve. The study session is what cements both the learning strategy and the learning session.

For many, challenges arise when the learning session is completed in isolation of the learning strategy and study session.

EIGHT

Study Habits To Unlock Potential

Let's look at the six study habits that will help you unlock the potential of your child.

The six habits

Schedule

It's a well-known adage that 'if you fail to plan, you plan to fail'. Time management is a key to success. To maximise your child's potential, create a schedule with them – one that includes time each week for recreation, family, exercise and, of course, homework and studying.

Sleep

Extensive research has identified that children who get adequate sleep see many benefits. They can recall information more easily, are more focused at school, behave better, maximise their learning and are healthier physically and mentally.

The American Academy of Paediatrics recommends that children should sleep the number of hours listed below:

- Infants under 1 year: 12–16 hours
- Children 1–2 years old: 11–14 hours
- Children 3–5 years old: 10–13 hours
- Children 6–12 years old: 9–12 hours

- Teenagers 13–18 years old: 8–10 hours[2]

Review of knowledge acquired

As discussed, there are three pillars of effective learning. One of them is the study session. If your child attends school but never reviews their classwork, they'll retain minimal information and the forgetting curve will be maximised. Effective revision involves actively reviewing new knowledge or skills throughout the learning process. Gaps in knowledge should be addressed when they're identified. Reviewing information the night before an exam isn't revision but cramming. Regular studying is necessary to unlock potential.

Study group

A study group is a group of students who meet regularly to delve deep into the knowledge

---

2 www.hopkinsallchildrens.org/ACH-News/General-News/The-importance-of-sleep-for-kids

they've acquired. There are great benefits to taking part in these groups. By joining a study group, your child can:

1. Optimise learning, since teaching is a great tool to identify the areas you have understood while uncovering gaps in knowledge
2. Fill in gaps in their knowledge
3. Learn new study habits
4. Build accountability with other group members
5. Develop intrinsic motivation and a healthy drive to succeed

Past papers

Past papers are an integral part of any revision endeavour. They should be used at every level within the educational system. They're an excellent snapshot of strengths and developmental areas.

Past papers will help your child:

1. Understand the layout of an exam paper

2. Identify common terminology and vocabulary

3. Improve their time-management skills (a great rule of thumb is to allocate one minute for each mark awarded in an exam)

4. Improve their comprehension skills

5. Build confidence in their test-taking ability

When your child has learned a topic, you can gather exam questions that relate to this topic and work through them together. This will help build resilience, self-esteem and confidence in your child.

Nutrition

Extensive research has linked diet and academic performance.[3] It's imperative to ensure your children are eating a balanced diet that will support and enhance their academic performance.

---

3   M.D. Florence, MSc, PDt, M. Asbridge, PhD, P.J. Veugelers, PhD, 'Diet Quality and Academic Performance', *Journal of School Health*, Volume 78, Issue 4, 2008. https://www.ncbi.nlm.nih.gov/pubmed/18336680

NINE

Navigating The Educational Maze

Some parents would describe the British educational system as a maze. What's frustrating about a maze is that there often appears to be many ways to reach the prize at the centre of it, but most paths don't lead to it. How many times have you journeyed down an educational path thinking it was leading you to a particular outcome only to find you were on the wrong path?

A tutor can hold your hand as you walk through the educational maze and help you reduce this frustration. There are several key milestones when it comes to education. If effective planning is undertaken at each milestone, you will unlock infinite potential in your child.

Key milestones

Application for primary school

Check the application process for a reception place at a primary school no later than the September of the year before they will be starting school (in September).

Planning ahead is a good idea when considering a primary school for your child. Here are some things to consider:

1. What is the school's educational philosophy?

2. What is the learning environment like at the school?

3. How does the prospective school foster parent partnership?

4. What does the latest OFSTED (Office for Standards in Education, Children's Services and Skills) report say about it?

Year 2 and Year 6 SATs

The Standard Assessment Tests (SATs) are a tool used to assess students in relation to national standards. Students complete their SATs in May of Year 2 (end of Key Stage One) and Year 6 (end of Key Stage Two) and receive their results in July.

They are assessed in reading, writing, mathematics and science and will be deemed to be working at greater depth within the expected standard, working at the expected standard, working towards the expected standard, working at the foundations for the expected standard or working below the standard of the Pre-Key Stage.

Eleven-plus

If your child is thinking about doing their eleven-plus, it's a good idea to have them start by the end of Year 3 or the beginning of Year 4.

To complete the eleven-plus, your child will need to be proficient in Key Stage 2 English and Maths and have a solid knowledge of Verbal Reasoning (VR) and Non-Verbal Reasoning (NVR).

Application for secondary school

Secondary school applications should be completed no later than April of the year your child will start secondary school.

Things to consider when looking for a secondary school for your child (again, planning ahead is a good idea):

1. What is the school's educational philosophy?

2. What is the learning environment like at the school?

3. How does the prospective school foster parent partnership?

4. What does the latest OFSTED (Office for Standards in Education, Children's Services and Skills) report say about it?

Year 9 options

Options are designed to empower your child to think about potential careers and choose subjects that are aligned with their prospective career pathway.

Tips for choosing options:

1. Begin with the end in mind – encourage your child to think about what careers they're interested in

2. Encourage them to choose subjects that will provide a foundation for further study

Year 10 GCSEs

The shift from Key Stage 3 (Year 7 until Year 9) to Key Stage 4 (Year 10 until Year 11) is a big one. The skills used in Key Stage 3 will need to be developed in Key Stage 4, so your child can unlock their potential.

Robust study habits will be even more necessary now, and they will put your child in a good position to pass their GCSEs.

TEN

Triad Partnership Model

A parental partnership is a working relationship between parent, child and school. The effectivity of this relationship largely depends on the school, parent and child working together in a harmonious way.

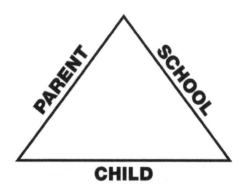

School involvement

The school involvement in the parental partnership is key. It will facilitate the unlocking of potential in your child. The school can:

- Provide parents with newsletters
- Hold regular parent meetings to discuss children's academic progress throughout the year

- Provide an online parent portal, where parents can access their children's progress and communicate with teachers
- Provide parent surveys

Parent involvement

There are many ways parents can be involved in this partnership:

- Become a parent governor to stay informed about the school's decision-making processes.
- Help enforce the school's vision, mission and ethos.
- Support your children with their homework.
- Communicate with your child's school via their school planner.

- Ensure your child attends school, the statutory expectation is at least 95% attendance.

While parent-school partnerships significantly improve student performance, I can show you a better way. A partnership between parent, school and tutor is comprised of three cords that can't be broken. The child will sit at the centre of this partnership triad, which will strategically unlock their potential.

Tutor involvement

A good tutor will:

- Identify your child's learning style and provide a strategic plan to accelerate the unlocking of your child's potential.
- Help you navigate the educational maze.

- Support you in the basics of literacy and numeracy, so you're empowered to support your child at home.

- Help you build a routine with your child.

- Provide a sounding board that will leave you feeling focused and clear.

- Teach your child study skills that foster a positive self-concept.

Seven principles of effective triad partnership

1. Strategic planning to unlock the child's potential must include parent, school and tutor.

2. All communication must be relevant to unlocking potential.

3. All parties must be kept up to date on relevant information.

4. Parents must be involved with all the tutor's and the school's activities.

5. An empowering environment that fosters connection and cultivation must be created.

6. Parents' questions and concerns must be addressed.

7. All parties involved must be accountable.

ELEVEN

Top Tips For Finding A Tutor

A recent survey revealed that one in four children has had tuition in their school career.[4] If you're considering working with a tutor or an established tuition centre, here are a few tips to keep in mind.

---

4   www.suttontrust.com/newsarchive/private-tuition-still
    -common-for-secondary-school-pupils

Look for enthusiasm

How successfully knowledge is passed on to a child is largely dependent on the enthusiasm the tutor has for teaching. Enthusiasm can transform a highly unmotivated child who despises learning into a highly motivated child who wants to learn.

A passionate tutor can make even the most tedious topic relevant and interesting. And most importantly, they can empower your child to overcome their learning hurdles and make incremental progress.

Ask yourself if your tutor shows enthusiasm for teaching.

Look for professionalism

Central to effective tuition is the professional relationship developed and sustained between tutor, parent and child. This relationship will underpin all tuition efforts.

It's important that the prospective tutor is able to make your child feel comfortable and to help them build intrinsic motivation. Your child needs to feel they can ask questions and that they'll be supported, not ridiculed. If a tutor cannot form a solid working relationship with your child, it's unlikely your child will progress quickly.

The relationship developed over time between the tutor and your child will determine the learning environment. If the relationship is negative, the learning environment will also be negative. If the relationship is positive, the learning environment will be as well – and a positive learning environment will accelerate the unlocking of potential.

It's also important for the tutor to form a healthy relationship with you, the parent/carer, and that they provide you with regular updates (this is covered more in tip six).

Three questions to ask your prospective tutor:

- How have you formed professional relationships with your current students?

- How do you create a positive learning environment?

- How do you intend on unlocking the potential in my child?

Consider the tutor's philosophy

The prospective tutor's philosophy around education generally and tuition specifically will largely impact the way tuition is delivered to your child. For example, does the prospective tutor believe knowledge should be imparted in a fun, engaging way? Is the prospective tutor prepared to go the extra mile to unlock the potential in your child?

Consider the tutor's credibility

It would be disastrous to use the services of a tutor with no prior experience working with a child like yours, so it's important to establish these things:

- What teaching qualifications and/or experience does the prospective tutor have?

- What are their pass rates?

- Have they worked with a child like yours before?

Consider legislation

The prospective tutor *must* comply with legislation and statutory guidelines. It's worthwhile to request the following documentation:

- Professional references and/or testimonials – these things will help you decide whether they're suitable to work with children

- Disclosure and Barring Service (DBS) check – your prospective tutor must have had a DBS check, which will tell you whether they have a criminal conviction that would render them unsuitable to work with children (it's good practice for tuition centre to have on display a list of all team members employed in the tuition centre)

- Insurance – all tutors must have appropriate insurance coverage, including public liability and professional indemnity

- Photographic ID – to ensure the person in front of you is the person they have declared themselves to be

NB: If your prospective tutor works independently, they should provide you with the above documentation. If your prospective tutor works for a tuition centre, the centre should adhere to a safer recruitment policy.

Make sure they're willing to provide regular tuition updates

Regular tuition updates empower parents by keeping them 'in the know'. You will become more confident as you engage with the tutor. An effective tuition update should include:

- The tuition objective – it's important to be aware of what your child has learned in the lesson, so the tuition update should include a brief outline of the session

- Identified developmental areas – good tutors will have an accurate view of their tutee's learning strengths and developmental areas; the update should show you which developmental areas to focus on with your child

- A way forward – your tutor should be able to clearly articulate how they plan to support your child in their developmental areas

Make sure your goals match theirs

It's important to be clear about your goals for your child's tuition. What are you hoping to see achieved? Can the prospective tutor help you with this? If you (or your tutor) are unclear on what's needed, how will you be able to measure progress?

It may be worth considering these points:

- Will your tutor offer an assessment to determine areas of strengths and development areas?

- How will the tutor monitor and review your child's progress (ie the unlocking of their potential)?

- How will the prospective tutor support you and your child in achieving your goals for the tuition?

Tuition is an effective tool to maximise the unlocking of potential in your child. But its effectiveness is linked to the tutor. The seven tips outlined here will provide you with a framework for finding a tutor that's right for you and your child.

SECTION THREE

THE EMPOWERING MINDSET

How many times are children asked the famous question: 'When you're older, what would you like to be?' Many parents hope their child will choose a highly respected job that pays well (eg doctor, lawyer, accountant). If the child states a preference for a career that's less desirable (eg athlete, hairstylist), the parents may encourage them to choose something that will give them more financial security or societal respect.

We (parents, carers, teachers, etc) naturally want the best for the next generation, and subconsciously, we project our fears onto our children. We give them all the reasons why they can't achieve success in a certain career.

TWELVE

Persuasion

The persuasions of the adults in their life largely impact children positively or negatively. Our persuasion sets the tone for the environment we create and sustain for our children. What sorts of things are you imprinting on your child? Have you imprinted your insecurities on them? Are you seeking to live out your life goals through them? Have you made mistakes that you hope to correct through their life? Whatever the case may be, it's important to stand back and examine how you're persuading your child.

When we ask our children that famous question, it's our responsibility to facilitate the unlocking of potential. We must help them identify their purpose. This will be covered in more detail later.

Occupational paradigm

Our persuasions will shape the kinds of adults our children become. And when we imprint our fear-based persuasions on our children (eg 'seek a good education and get a good job that pays a good salary so you'll have financial security'), we miss the point. We are operating with an outside-in approach, rather than an inside-out approach. We are operating out of alignment with our true selves – with our life purpose.

The outside-in approach is referred to as the occupational paradigm. 'Occupation' comes from the Latin word *occupationem*, which means 'taking possession; business, employment'.

Therefore, someone who favours the occupational paradigm will take possession of a financial vehicle (ie a job, a business, or investment opportunity) for the sole purpose of attaining financial security.

This person will see their role in society as one of transaction facilitator. In other words, 'I will serve society to make money'. These people will reach a time in their life when they begin to feel empty and will question the reason for their existence.

There's nothing wrong with seeking an awesome lifestyle – nice house, nice cars, etc. But at what price? Will the quest to attain status symbols satisfy your hunger for a rewarding life? Will the quest for success satisfy your soul?

You are designed for greatness. Your children and all who are connected to you are designed for greatness. You hold a unique blueprint for greatness – one that only you possess. Yes, only you!

People who live according to the occupational paradigm will forever set goals that aren't congruent with their true values. Outwardly, their results will look impressive. They may receive accolades, awards or societal respect, but inwardly they desire more. More fulfilment. More of what they were born to do.

Are you doing what you were born to do? Do you know what you were born to do?

Children who are parented according to the Disempowering Parenting Model are likely to favour the occupational paradigm. They are likely to need validation from society to feel as if they've attained success. They will continue shaping themselves according to how they are perceived by others because they don't understand the importance of internal validation.

Does any of the above resonate with you?

Now consider this checklist. People who operate from the occupational paradigm tend to:

1. Believe that Monday is the worst day of the week

2. Always count down the days to the next holiday

3. Feel like one hour lasts an eternity

4. Believe that wealth follows being well-paid

5. Ask: 'How can the world serve me, myself and I?'

6. Always be looking for new ventures to make more money

7. Count down the years to pension age

8. Conform to societal values and norms

I can show you a much better approach: the inside-out approach, referred to as the vocational paradigm.

Vocational paradigm

In Latin, 'vocation' is *vocare*, which means 'to call'. In essence, to live according to a vocational paradigm is to live in alignment with our calling, our true selves.

Within each of us is a unique blend of gifts and talents, which help us create our story. Our gifts and talents allow us to unlock our life purpose so we can fulfil what we were called to do: what we were born to do. If you said to me, 'I have no story!' I wouldn't believe you. You have a unique story that only you can tell.

You are uniquely designed with gifts so you can serve the world, transform lives and make an impact on generations to come.

When we favour the vocational paradigm, we listen intently to our true selves. This listening enables us to serve the world using our gifts. Those who live according to the vocational paradigm are always asking themselves, 'How can I better serve the world?'

People who operate from the vocational paradigm tend to:

1.   Believe that Monday is the best day of the week
2.   Feel like one hour lasts five minutes
3.   Be excited about making a lasting impact on generations to come
4.   Believe that wealth follows impact
5.   Ask, 'How can I serve the world?'

The core of our life is manifested in every facet of our lives. The primary objective of those who live by the occupational paradigm is to make money to maintain or build an ideal lifestyle, while the primary objective of those who live by the vocational paradigm is to live as their true selves and leave a legacy.

People who live by the vocational paradigm are fulfilled, as they spend their time focusing on things they're concerned and passionate about. When you live your life according to the vocational paradigm, you will become a magnet – opportunities will flow in your direction.

THIRTEEN

Unlocking Purpose

The way we persuade our children is based on whether we prefer the occupational paradigm or the vocational paradigm. The vocational paradigm is superior, as it allows us to empower our children to develop an unquenchable thirst to find their life purpose.

Passion (ie excitement) and purpose go hand in hand. Underneath our passions is our life purpose. We can peel back our passions as if they're layers of an onion – they are the layers of our life purpose.

Parents have a responsibility to help their children unlock this purpose. They need to enable their children to focus on their life purpose, and this is more easily accomplished when they live according to a vocational paradigm.

Seven steps to unlocking your child's life purpose

1. Guide your child to discover what they're passionate about and what challenges them

2. Have resources available that are related to these passions and challenges

3. Encourage your child to write in a journal about what excites and challenges them

4. Enrol them in classes that are relevant to their passions

5. Support your child by acknowledging their gifts and talents

6. Encourage your child to clarify their values

7. Help them write a powerful life purpose statement

FOURTEEN

Resources

Your potential is tied to your perception. Perception is the basis of a person's psychology (how they think about and understand the world).

Your perception has the power to elevate you to new heights or to keep you within the realms of the status quo. If you wear glasses, your sight will be as good as the glasses allow. If you wear the wrong prescription, you'll have diminished eyesight and won't be able to see everything around you. Similarly, your perception largely determines what you see as possible, or impossible.

You've likely heard the phrase 'show me your friends and I'll know who you are'. External support in the form of a life coach or mentor will help you challenge your current perception. These professionals can help you perceive as possible things you previously deemed impossible.

Depending on where you are in your career, you may need external support to accelerate your professional development. If you favour the vocational paradigm, you serve people through your gifts. How efficient you are in doing so and the number of people you serve will largely determine the salary you can expect to earn. The better you become at serving with sincerity and passion, the more earning potential you'll have. The occupational paradigm will take you only so far – the vocational paradigm will allow you to make a lasting impact and help your earning potential skyrocket.

External support will help you unlock this professional potential.

Two vehicles to unlock your professional potential

Life coach

The life coach has an empowering relationship with their client, supporting their clients to unlock their potential and to see their life vision as clearly as possible. They help to develop a strategic plan to bring this vision to fruition and to raise performance through this truth with accountability and support.

The seven key benefits of working with a life coach are:

1. Support to accelerate the realisation of strategic plans with accountability

2. Increased confidence as the life coach empowers the client to work through limiting beliefs

3. A sounding board for limitless possibilities

4. Clarity around life purpose and how this relates to your life vision

5. Increased congruence due to increased awareness of your values

6. Greater work–life balance through self-discovery of what is important

7. Greater productivity as you align yourself to your gifts and talents

Mentorship

Mentoring is an empowering relationship through which the (more experienced) mentor passes on valuable knowledge and skills in a safe learning space to unlock their (less experienced) mentee's potential to raise their performance.

The seven key benefits of a mentor are that they enable you to:

1. Develop a reflective practice

2. Gain feedback on strengths and developmental areas

3. Access their mentor network

4. Learn from the pitfalls and successes of someone with more experience

5. A springboard for problem-solving skills and encouragement

6. Expert guidance on professional development

7. Increase personal and professional performance

FIFTEEN

Purpose Development Programme

Central to the vocational paradigm is serv-anthood. A successful person understands the importance of serving others. Outstanding results are achieved when a pursuit adds value to the world.

To maximise your impact, it's important to review your success model through a purpose audit, a career plan and a career evaluation (these will be addressed in Chapter Nineteen).

This will help you identify development areas. You can then complete a purpose development programme to address these areas. This will enable you to serve more effectively.

Education is an empowering tool that will help you develop your gifts and talents. It's not a destination (ie degrees) but a vehicle. A vehicle takes its passengers to many different locations. It's designed for journeys. In the same way, different kinds of education will take you to different places, different results. It's your responsibility to choose the education vehicle that will sharpen your gifts and talents so you can serve the world with more passion, empathy and excellence.

The right education will help bring forth your talents and gifts. It will improve your knowledge, understanding and skills so you can better serve your sphere of influence. It will nourish your soul and draw out the best in you.

In serving others, you must be clear about the problem you're solving. You are remunerated for your ability to solve it, to provide a solution. How well you solve problems will determine whether you're in high demand. You must constantly seek to improve yourself – to become the best version of you.

Great leaders have a common denominator: they can clearly explain their life purpose. Their influence (ability to draw a following) is largely based on their ability to achieve the desired results linked to their purpose.

A vibrant career always starts with a why: 'Why was I created?' Then, to become an effectual leader in your sphere of influence, you must ask how: 'How can I serve effectively?'

SIXTEEN

Outstanding Work Ethic

Your work ethic is the psychology of smart working, servanthood and intrinsic motivation to succeed.

A good work ethic is the foundation of lasting success

Our work ethic is our psychology around how we use our gifts and talents. It either works for us or against us. Have you ever wondered why so many gifted, talented people never seem to attain success while others do? It's all about work ethic.

How you perceive work is a result of your belief system. When you have a solid work ethic, your talents and gifts work for you, and opportunities come your way (largely as a result of your reputation).

A good work ethic builds an amazing reputation

If asked to choose between more money and an exemplary reputation, most people would choose more money. But money is the fruit of a plant, not the root. The roots of a plant provide the nourishment necessary for fruit to thrive. Money is the result of your impact, which is underpinned by your work ethic.

A solid work ethic built over time will allow you to create a reputation for achieving exceptional results. You'll become known as a person who has integrity, who works hard, who is passionate, etc. And money follows this kind of reputation.

Money is the fruit of the matter while reputation is the root of the matter. If we don't like the fruit (what we get in exchange for the impact we've made), then it's time to address our reputation.

Ingredients of a good work ethic

A good work ethic has four key ingredients:

A 'sharp axe'

Let's consider two types of people: Person A and Person B.

Person A is attempting to cut down a tree. In the process, they exert a lot of energy. It takes them two hours to cut down the tree.

Person B cuts down the tree in fifteen minutes with little energy exerted.

How did Person B achieve this? The answer is found in the axe. Person A simply started working without preparation, while Person B took the time to sharpen their axe.

When we take time for strategic planning, risk analysis, acquiring more knowledge, building good relationships and reflecting, we 'sharpen the axe' and work smarter.

Do you take the time to sharpen your axe?

A commitment to servanthood

A tried-and-tested principle states: 'The greatest among you will be the servant'. A person of influence understands that in serving others, they make themselves great.

By approaching your work with an attitude of servanthood, you ensure you serve the world with your gifts and talents.

Application of knowledge

We must apply what we know to our work performance. And as part of working smart, we must identify what education will help us sharpen our axe.

An intrinsic motivation to succeed

Motivation can be either extrinsic or intrinsic. Intrinsic motivation stems from passion: passion to serve the world, to ensure our life purpose is manifested. It stems from a burning passion to see our potential fully realised. When the going gets tough, it's intrinsic motivation that will spur you on.

Seven characteristics of someone with a good work ethic

1. They produce high-quality work (consistently)

2. They present themselves professionally, both in terms of their appearance and how they communicate

3. They value teamwork and cooperation

4. They are determined to succeed, despite obstacles

5. They have integrity and can be trusted

6. They have confidence

7. They engage in continuing professional development, knowing that they can progress only as far as their knowledge

SEVENTEEN

Success

Success means different things to different people. To some, success is having a high bank balance, raising their children to exceed their achievements, or attaining status symbols (ie the big house and fancy car). But we can have all these things and feel empty. Why? Because true success isn't a destination but a journey of self-discovery. When you unlock your purpose, and your purpose becomes your reality – this is true fulfilment, true success.

Achieving true success involves digging deep to understand your purpose. To achieve great things but never fulfil your purpose would be a tragedy! True success isn't about reaching milestones that society deems important. Rather, it's an inward achievement. You will have achieved true success when you're maximising your potential; you will understand your unique blend of gifts and talents and be aligned with your purpose daily. You will be concerned with how to make a lasting impact on society.

Your success isn't something that can be compared to others', and it isn't fuelled by jealousy.

How you choose to define success affects the way in which you manage your time. And how we manage our time is the biggest predictor of our future success. Good success is the by-product of understanding the principles that govern success. This means when the words we speak align with this quest, together with our subconscious thinking. Our subconscious thinking is a further indicator of whether we'll be successful in the future.

Success model

Purpose audit

You were created with a unique design, with a unique blend of gifts and talents. These gifts and talents are what I refer to as 'purpose enablers'.

To adopt the vocational paradigm is to adopt a certain way of thinking. Your subconscious thinking shapes the type of life you live. At its core, people who live according to the vocational paradigm are people-centred and seek to serve others with passion, conviction and excellence.

And these people regularly assess their purpose – they do a purpose audit. They understand first-hand that to be fulfilled and make an impact, they must be self-aware and identify what they're naturally good at.

Career plan

Most of us spend one-third of our waking hours at work, so it's important to choose a career that is aligned with your purpose. Your work shouldn't be simply an exchange of time for money.

A career plan always starts with a life vision. Your life vision is your purpose in pictures. It clearly shows the end point you're aiming for. Seeing is believing – you must first see your vision and then use self-awareness to develop a career plan that will take you from point A (your life vision) to point B (your goal). Success leaves clues. Every successful person understands the importance of planning their career in terms of building a foundation for lasting success.

Career evaluation

In life, it's easy to become stagnant and complacent, to coast until the next endeavour comes along. But true success involves asking yourself, 'How can I serve better? How can I maximise my impact on society? How can I impact lives, one person at a time?' The success model is rooted in the vocational paradigm.

Career evaluation is a tool to help you sharpen your axe. If you use the same axe for twenty years and never sharpen it, it will become blunt.

What once rendered powerful results will no longer be impactful. Sharpening the axe means asking the questions above. By taking the time to do so, you will yield great results. It can be done as a selfless act if you do so with the intention of exploring how you can serve others better. Who among you is the greatest? The one who understands the importance of serving.

EIGHTEEN

Execution

The purpose model is an empowering tool. It has several components:

1. **Persuasion – identifying your paradigm.**
   Identify whether you're operating according to the occupational paradigm or the vocational paradigm.

   The vocational paradigm is the better choice, as it will empower you to identify your purpose and seek a career that will give your purpose expression.

2. **Unlocking – the seven-step process to unlock your child's life purpose.** Empower your child to discover their passions, which are indicators of their purpose. Your child's gifts and talents are tools that will help them see their purpose come to life.

3. **Resources – the two advisors who help you plan for success.** Accelerate the unlocking of your child's potential through the strategic use of two resources: coaches and mentors. They will help your child's plan to be successful.

4. **Programme – education to sharpen your gifts and talents.** Serve others effectively by developing your knowledge, skills and competence through education.

5. **Outstanding work ethic – a work ethic that will set your child apart.** Help your child develop a solid work ethic, as no

talent or gift will produce lasting results without one.

6. **Success – potential is the measure of your child's purpose.** Look within and not without when defining your success. Don't compare your achievements with others'. Looking within means you're constantly reviewing your potential in relation to your purpose.

7. **Execution – taking action.** Execute to see results. The first six pillars of the purpose model won't yield results if you don't take action. Execution will take you from the realm of knowledge to the realm of application. Wisdom is the principal thing. Wisdom is the ability to correctly apply the first six pillars of the purpose model to your life, and doing so will give you clarity, direction and a sense of fulfilment.

In simple terms, 'execution' is the ability to do what's required of you in relation to the purpose model. Effective execution is dependent on strategy, accountability and self-discipline.

Strategy

Strategy equals clarity. Clarity comes from a place of beginning with the end in mind. You must be able to visualise your goal and then determine the actions required to make the goal become a reality. Execution without strategy is a sure recipe for disaster.

Accountability

Accountability is a vital ingredient of successful execution. Seek expertise from people who have a proven track record in the pillar you're seeking to cultivate.

Self-discipline

Motivation will lead you through the door of opportunity, but self-discipline will keep you on the other side. To see lasting success, you need more than simply a desire to change. Self-discipline means taking action on a pillar irrespective of how you feel. Self-discipline ensures you'll be taking action over the long term.

Acknowledgements

To my empowering parents, Vivienne M Hall (Mum) and Winston D Hall (Dad): I am eternally thankful that, despite being diagnosed with dyslexia at the tender age of three, statemented and four years behind my peers, you saw my potential. You both encouraged me, supported me and gave me the guidance to be the man I am today, thank you. Much love.

To my empowering wife, Natalie N Hall: I thank you for seeing my potential. We have journeyed through some lovely mountain tops and some valleys, but through it all we are committed to unlocking each other's potential. I love you with all my heart.

To my amazing daughter, Hannah E Hall: I am so proud of you and honoured to be your daddy. You are my WHY; you have changed my life in so many ways to be your empowering daddy. As long as I am on Earth, I am committed to unlocking your potential. Your daddy loves you.

The Author

David C Hall is a qualified science teacher with eleven years' experience in a range of school environments. His philosophy is that your child can succeed. After being diagnosed as dyslexic at the age of three and struggling throughout primary school, David developed a routine, the work ethic and confidence to set and achieve goals. He left his secondary school with ten GCSE passes at grades A* to C.

He set up Potential Unlocked Tuition in Birmingham as a centre where children will flourish in a nurturing, supportive and stimulating learning environment. They have unlocked the potential in over 250 children in the past two years, and have featured in *The Voice* newspaper and in Birmingham Live.

You can contact David at:

🌐 www.davidchall.co.uk

📞 0121 405 1983

Lightning Source UK Ltd.
Milton Keynes UK
UKHW020629280421
382760UK00007B/149

9 781781 334157